Medicine Show

TOM YUILL

Medicine Show

THE UNIVERSITY OF CHICAGO PRESS

Chicago & London

TOM YUILL is lecturer in liberal arts at Metropolitan College, Boston University, and associate professor of literature and creative writing at the New England Institute of Art.

The University of Chicago Press, Chicago 60637
The University of Chicago Press, Ltd., London
© 2010 by The University of Chicago
All rights reserved. Published 2010
Printed in the United States of America
19 18 17 16 15 14 13 12 11 10   1 2 3 4 5

ISBN-13: 978-0-226-97164-3 (cloth)
ISBN-13: 978-0-226-97165-0 (paper)
ISBN-10: 0-226-97164-3 (cloth)
ISBN-10: 0-226-97165-1 (paper)

Library of Congress Cataloging-in-Publication Data
Yuill, Tom.
    Medicine Show / Tom Yuill.
        p. cm. — (Phoenix poets)
    ISBN-13: 978-0-226-97164-3 (hardcover : alk. paper)
    ISBN-10: 0-226-97164-3 (hardcover : alk. paper)
    ISBN-13: 978-0-226-97165-0 (pbk. : alk. paper)
    ISBN-10: 0-226-97165-1 (pbk. : alk. paper)
    I. Title.
    PS3625.U35M43 2010
    813'.11—dc22   2009034328

♾ The paper used in this publication meets the minimum requirements of the American National Standard for Information Sciences—Permanence of Paper for Printed Library Materials, ANSI Z39.48-1992.

for LESLIE LEE

CONTENTS

ACKNOWLEDGMENTS

I want to thank the editors of the following journals in which these poems, sometimes in different versions, first appeared:

Literary Imagination: The Review of the Association of Literary Scholars and Critics: "Medicine Show" (page 21), "Fragment"
Naked Truth: "Debate with His Heart" (earlier version)
The New Journal: "Lovers"
A Public Space: "Coyote," "Debate with His Heart" (later version), "Several Histories," "Dallas Skinheads" (shorter version)
Salamander: "It Happens"

I am grateful for the support of a Teaching Fellowship and numerous successive teaching appointments at Boston University.

I wish to thank for their invaluable support Julia Yuill Harkins; R. Wayne and Francis Nunnally; the Honorable Lydia Calvert Taylor; Dr. Paige Frazer; Hal Yuill; John Yuill; my sisters, Catherine and Margaret; and my parents, Joan and Charles.

Many thanks to the poets whose insight and generosity helped me write this book, particularly Derek Walcott, Rosanna Warren, David Ferry, Peter Campion, Tim Seibles, Scott Cairns, and David Blair.

I owe a special debt of gratitude to Robert Pinsky.

Every Wolf's and Lion's howl
Raises from Hell a Human Soul.

William Blake, *Auguries of Innocence*

COYOTE

My friend, I could wander
Around out here for years,
Shaking my head for letting him out,
Swearing not to forgive myself
If anything should happen.
He slipped out in the rain
While I slept. I followed,
Desperate, with a picture, asking people,
Have you seen this coyote?
He went across the ocean
On a freight ship, sat in the corners
Of doorways on Rue Montmartre,
On Aston Quay, and in London,
Slumped, head between his knees,
Longing for the familiar woods,
Longing for the last red glimpse of sun
On the lake. He says he is a coyote
Who does what he likes. He likes
To stay outside. Tonight under the evening
Clouds in their cold, silver raiment
He sits there, alone,
And I must go out to find him.

One

BIT: AN ODE WITH THE ROLLING STONES PLAYING IN THE BACKGROUND

The King squirms, on the spot.
Each remark makes a wound, like a mouth.
Each hot thought grins like a raccoon.
Each moment heats itself against another moment.

Each thing fucks. Each thing wants.
Waste and pain again and again.
They got me with a fine they didn't tell me was a fine.
They got people like teeth, whose job is being sharp.

"They got people dressed in plastic bags directing traffic."
Wake up, King! Wake up the Son of Man.
The sex between the sexes hasn't stopped.
The drinking of the drunkards hasn't stopped.

The King inspects his mud flaps, then anoints his beets.
Each mouth slobbers. Each mouth eats.

UNSOLICITED ELEGY

My brothers, the Wag and the Artful Dodger
(Really my cousins) awoke me at 3:44. We poured big
Bourbon and cokes and took a walk.

Traylor asked how my broken leg was healing,
I asked how his broken collar bone was healing.
Charles told us his plan: "I'll take biology,

And really study. Then, if I receive a B, I leave
The frat house, study all the time. It's med school.
I'm a doctor. If it's below a B, stay in the house,

It's business, I'm a millionaire from business."
What about B minus? "Still a B. I'm still
A doctor." And same goes for C plus? "It's not

A B. So I'm in business, Cousin." They wanted big
Aquariums. No matter what we talked about,
Charles had an answer, Traylor had philosophy

Like this: "If you're ever in a group
Of people longer than 15 minutes and can't figure
Out who the dumbass is, you're it." We listened

Once as a neighbor said he'd been to a big concert
Where most who showed up after him got in
For free. "But we were not ripped off," he said,

"Because we paid, the concert happened, everyone
Enjoyed it." Sure they said, and Gentleman Traylor
Glanced at me and grinned like a raccoon, just

For a second, as if to say, "we've found the dumbass,
Haven't we, Tom?" Ten years after the accident
Which I only survived by having missed, I said,

Voice shaking as I spoke to the 200 gathered
For the reunion what I'd written that morning
To Traylor and Charles. *"Because I was not there*

At Chamonix to save you, I will save you with poetry
For the rest of my life." So I swore ten years ago,
And for ten years now, they have helped save me.

LOVERS

The air is hot, it whispers, it has lips.
It whispers like good news . . . *the beer is cold.*
She lumbers for one more. "Eywhere'd she go?"
He thinks, but turns and thinks, "oh there she is."

He's sitting by her on the floor with lime-
Peels, open tubes of paint; some Jonathan
Richman's playing. One of them's been painting.
Dos Equis are being knocked back. He finds

He knows where she is. She sees him. It's summer,
They're on the floor. The music's like good news.
"I get a facial tic when I drink too
Much Coke," he says. "Each time I brush

My teeth I think about Wisconsin," she nods.
They whisper, purse their lips, it's all good news.

ODE TO THE WIND

I'm older now and live without regard
For consequences less than in my youth.
And I don't like you stuffing my nose

Full of sewery rain, whipping swill
Around corners and overfed pillars.
I do like the way you make the trees rattle,

A soundtrack around me, or lover-
Like presence, for which I am grateful, if I am
Lonely. But I have to say, it annoys

Me that you blow, or that you're blown,
That you don't emerge from some *regard*.
What? Don't say I'm out of line.

I still know about influences, flux
Of "swirl and vortex." "Weather." Hey, I *choose*
To walk this way, I *choose*

To stand here being blown by you.
And though you bring me
New ideas for lunch—tacos *al carbon*

Or crispy sesame beef—you also piss
Careeningly all over me
Without regard. This isn't envy here.

I know you, Dog. I've seen you
Knock the stuffing from the sea, and
I've been blown before. Bring it.

FOR ORLEANS
Villon

Here beside the fountain I die of thirst.
In my own state I'm in a foreign land.
I'm comforted and grin when in despair.
When dolled up like a judge, bare as a wurst.
I talk about my pleasures but they're bland.
I'm always welcomed, always shown the door.

At daybreak I tell all good night, good luck.
All my learning's earned by pure, blind chance.
While lying down I know I'll fall. I'm sure.
I'm so well set I don't have one sawbuck.
Am not an heir, expect inheritance,
Am always welcomed, always shown the door.

I work, but still don't give a happy damn.
I'll spend my coins before I stop to think.
I know it all and my mind is a blur,
Lies, the truth—to me they're both the same.
It's soothing knowing the sturdiest boat sinks.
I'm always welcomed, always shown the door.

Forbearing Princes, learn: I know the score.
I'm quite unique, like everyone you've known.
What's my gift? Retrieving things I pawn,
Being always welcomed, always shown the door.

TWO EASY ODES

1. ODE TO THE MOON

I sit up and see the moon at night.
It is right there past my nose. The bright

Half-tortilla, she brings scrambled eggs to mind.
I'm chirped at by thoughts when I sit up and see

The moon. I'm not here waiting for the smacking
Sun. I roll up in a world that licks its chops

And thumps around me, sometimes stubs my toes.
(But I wouldn't turn around and hate you,

World, I learn to love you by the hoist and drop.)
I do my sit-ups, curling and uncurling, I am half

A somersault, just like the moon this night.
Back and forth go the tides. I curl in,

I go out. I close my eyes almost
And there's my nose. Back and forth, there's my nose,

There's my knees, there they go. Let's have eggs
On flour tortillas. You and me, Moon: you and me.

2. ODE FROM MY HEART

Broken, fixed, and drunk with love, I go,
I gasp, I peak, I spin. I'm lodged but loose
And chuckling. Glottal thumping—that's me.

I gape, I eat the filaments from distant
Vistas coming in a rhythmic rush
And poop them out. I am the throbbing

World. I shiver for you, but I am a purring
World as well. I bloom, I push the papery
Clouds around me. I live in my vault and love

And punch the ribbed claw that fixes me. I don't stop.
I hoist, I drop, soothe, I shower, rush, peruse. I breathe,
I weep, I plop, I try. I ring, chime, coo, sing, do.

THE BLUE-EYED GIANT, THE MINIATURE WOMAN, AND THE HONEYSUCKLE

freely after Hikmet

He was a blue-eyed giant.
He loved a miniature woman.
The woman's dream was a miniature house
    With a miniature mortgage, dork
    For a husband, but honeysuckle
    Growing, a riot of colors, very fine house.

The giant loved like a giant,
Loved the giant world, its giant feet of clay.
His head was accustomed to such giant ideas
That the giant kept seeing the faces of fathers,
    Of Washington and Crazy Horse, in damned
    Near every cloud. If she yelled at him he nearly
    Snapped. Damn couch legs were prison bars.

He loved like a giant. His desires were few, but those
He had he had lots of. He could not knock
On the door before something of himself was already
Through it. Could not fit in a miniature house,
    Could not be a dork with a miniature mortgage
    In a house where honeysuckle grows
    In a riot of colors.

He stayed a blue-eyed giant. He loved the miniature
Woman. She was a porcelain miniature of a miniature
Woman. The woman was hungry for miniature prose.
She needed a comfortable sectional couch,
 She got tired of the giant's long strides, his almost
 Snapping when he stubbed his toe, and, bye, bye, off
 She went to a dwarf with a mortgaged, miniature

Future, no questions and, sure, a garden
With some honeysuckle growing in a riot of color.
Now the blue-eyed giant knows there is no grave
For a giant's loves. No memory permitted for the love
 Of one who sees faces in clouds, of one who loves
 Like a giant, no recollection of him in the miniature
 Houses whose gardens grow honeysuckle
 In the standard riot of colors.

HER CHOIR

pomegranate

     adored one

the sky filled with snow

  swirling

her hips as she turns in bed
to face me

     a swirling and a whiteness

that fill the sky—

  for Heaven to be

all of it must be
all at once—

pomegranate

    white hips   she
  turning adored one

   toward me

DALLAS SKINHEADS

Heads shaved to give advantage during fist-
Fights at soccer games in Manchester or

Berlin became shaved heads in Addison or
Farmer's Branch, decorticated smooth to piss

On both "Thou Shalt" and "Thou Shalt Not."
Oh, skinheads of the early eighties, yes, you had

A weird joie de vivre. Stomping and
Swinging with torpid disinterest. Bloodshot

Eyes crossing from indifferent headbutting
Of windshields and indifferent gobbling of

Acid and Ecstacy. Not even drunken, wobbling love,
Just wanting whatever the next sting

Was. Oh, raspberries blown at ennui in the form
Of noses burst to bloom by redneck fists,

Were you mostly piss? Ah, Dionysus
In the eighties, hairspray paisleyed on bangs, storms

At dinner tables in St. Louis, in Ann Arbor.
Long sleeve paisley shirts covering tracks

In Plano. No to the bond salesman father, yes to smack
After dinner. The death rattle should be adored,

She'd think, if she had the words. Another Self
Recorded in London, in New York, gives her

Her words. Dreams yielding, death seekers voting for
Reagan again, her own words not shelved,

Just not there. Grandmother dies suddenly, and dying
Floats in beneath Mom's shoulder blades.

Then she starts to smoke again, in secret. No charades
From Dionysus last. In the eighties people heard no crying.

"Get six jolly cowboys to carry my coffin,
Get six dancehall maidens to bear up my pall.

Throw bunches of roses all over my coffin,
Roses to deaden the clods as they fall."

Heads without hair in the cancer ward. Under knit
Caps, under silk scarves. Under the wig she wore

As she said, "I love you, too," and, unsure,
Tried not to cry as she walked in quick polite

Steps toward the hospital door, and he saw this, he
Saw this, he saw this, then got in the car

To go on to the concert. Are teenagers'
Arguments a good idea or not? Hast thou

Made the ulcers your idea? The Dallas skinhead
I knew swapped an Escort radar detector he stole

At five pm for seven hits of acid, which, poor mole,
He dropped, rubbing his head.

"It's always something with you, John," said his Mom
To her husband of twenty-two years, and he,

Tuning his car, heard nothing. O Mimesis, flue
For thistly mote, pearly cell or bomb,

Or migrating idea. Was he just infected, a Hell of Thought
In which no thoughts were his? What sign of Christ

Within his poor scalped hand as he gazes at the light
Which shivers in the hollow, vacant lot?

Two

MEDICINE SHOW

They just do what they have to do in Texas.
Researchy and formulaic, husks of laughing hatred rolling up
In swarms of blood behind your eye. You were a magician, seeing
A BU undergrad cross-eyed with drink dancing alone, many moons
Tattooed on her left shoulder blade. See the future: sitting jobless
On her mothy couch, then in a Cadillac,
Vintage but with an antique peanut butter cup
Blossoming mold on her dash board. The words are in my mouth,
She says, they're in the air before I think. The last of four
Silkworms you dreamed would eat into your thigh. Such thoughts appear
Tonight only: another family death, blown like a new war, from Texas to you.

THE BLUE BALLOON

After Lowell's Saba

The one time I felt pretty good today
(Forgive me, Lord, for that excess),
You wouldn't believe what showed up and ruined it.
Not someone I'd loved and hadn't
Married looking white hot at Za Za's
With upsized boobies and a phallic
Zirconian rock on her finger—nope.
It was a little blue balloon, blue
Like the sky over Waxahachie
When Mom dropped us off with Grandmother
To visit. Heaven above Texas
Has never been more blue.
Houses so beset upon by light they seem to burn,
And strings of smoke slip from a charcoal
Grill. The blue balloon took flight
And flew beyond all things divine,
Escaped the thoughtless hand of the small boy
(Who cried under the crush of this new loss),
And flew between the Water Tower
And Big Boy Kip's Coffee and Pancake House,
Where I was killing time and gaping at the blue
Balloon, grieving as I watched it lift and dip . . .

THE TOAD

Corbiere

A lone, throat-grime song, a barfed sestina
In the vapid night, a filmy moon, gray
Like dying teeth, its sheen green splotchwork . . .

An echoed loogey hawk, leaping
From behind the glandy lily pads . . .
It's gone! It's not! there, in the breasty mud . . .

A toad! O Crappo, why so scared? We're Army,
I am all fidelity, your lieutenant. See the bald, foam-
Rubber headed poet, nightingale of muck. Ooog . . .

Brrraapp! He sings! It's horror—sure, but why?
Do you not see his gloamy eye meet yours? See
Now he slurps away. Quiet and cold, under his rock . . .

Goodnight . . . that toad down there . . . that's me.

BETWEEN 56 AND 57

Villon

Old. Your tutor's drooping. Liver
Spots, my eyes which were like slate
Are sausage-grey. Grinded, I still quiver
At the thought of it, but I'm no bait.
Guillemette, your tapestries won't answer
Bill collectors. Lying is their trade.
Devalued coins will get you better.

Pay attention, new glovestitcher,
Time for you to get it straight.
You too, Blanche, you hobbled cobbler.
Get what's there. It soon gets late.
Factory girl—tripping dancer,
Don't stay shy. You'll never rate.
Devalued coins would fare no better.

Help me and yourselves. He baits her—
Jean, not you. Not you. Life is just hate,
Just men between our legs. He hates her
Later. Kate, those memories of maid-
Hood really cost you so much more. He'll offer
What you'll never get. Life is a blade.
Devalued coins will fare no better.

"Girls, when you see me I ache.
Listen, but don't look. I'm just a specter.
Can't go back and circulate.
Devalued coins would fare no better."

GRIEF

Hikmet

Is this grief I feel
    These sunny winter days,
    The longing to be somewhere else—
    On the old bridge in Istanbul, for instance,
    Or drinking with the workers in Adana,
    In the mountains of Greece, or in China,
    Or next to her, who no longer loves me?

Or is this a trick
              Of my liver
    Have I just dreamed all this?
    Or is it loneliness again,
    Or the fact I'm getting close
              To fifty now?

Friend, in the upcoming verse
My grief
        Will tip-toe nimbly out,
            It will go back the way it came—
If only I could write this poem
Or get a little sleep,
If only I received a letter
Or once heard good news on the radio . . .

XI
Catullus

Furius, Aurelius, my friends—my brothers;
Whether Catullus pushes to India's extremes,
To the resonating Eastern shore, so splashed
With echoing waves,

Or out to the Hyrcanians or to the plush Arabians,
Or further, to the Scythians or to the quick draw Parthians,
Whether to the shores so rubbed and stained
By the seven-mouthed Nile,

Or further, to the Alps, to see
The monuments to Caesar's girth, or further,
To the haunted Gallic Rhine, the witch-like
Land of Britons—

I would travel anywhere, I'd do all else
The will of God required of me to see
These words bespattering my former lover's face:

Live underneath your lovers, live for lust!
A happy, swelling lust! Dish out three hundred fucks
At once. No love required—just happy, oily fucking
Rotting off each crotch.

And do not think of me, or my poor love,
Which died because of you, just as a meadow
Flower dies and falls after the sweeping past
Of the silent plow.

YOU WERE NOT HANGED, AND IT WAS NOT SCIENCE

She thought she had debased herself
Just as he'd asked. Gone to his therapist and listened
While he cried about his acid reflux. Hells of her own
Bad crying jags alone. Infected nails like dust mites,
Gathering between his thoughts. The therapist explained
He was a scientist, objective, and he'd seen a tennis game

Where he should see a game of building Legos.
Memory's the scapegoat. It's always
A memory that makes
The bile rise again. She listened and stared
Out the window, thinking, "I have a knife on me."
They plucked hairs from his head. He stared.

She wrinkled up right in her chair. "Just make yourselves
A deal," the Scientist went on, spreading his legs
And leaning back in his chair. "Let her look,"
He said, "at your new poems. Then we'll look
At what you think she thinks." Seventeen minutes
Went by. She recited "Directive" four times

In her head. If it's medical, then why not get to all
The truth, he asked himself. Why doesn't she say
Everything she knows is true that matters? Why doesn't
He say something, she thinks. He doesn't care, that's why.
In India one story was you rid your soul of viral steam
By spitting in a convict's hair. Armies on their way to war

March by to spit in the convict's hair. It worked as long
As no one ever felt the convict was mistreated.
All it took was one to think, this person's been
Mistreated, and confusion. Anybody might be wrong.
Hast thou not heard? Hast thou not understood?
They're arguing over what happened because

There is no memory except one they invent
And reinvent, and reinvent. What else do lovers do
But reinvent forever memories they can be happy with?
But therapists are like cocaine. If one is into it, the other
Must get into it or split. "You don't think this is science?"
It's just a shame the other thinks, feeling estranged.

CRYING

Hikmet

Freedom, for all your distrust.
Your lidded eyes stream, your mind,
Licked clean, can recline like a sky.
Freedom like rain. Nothing to trust.

Like a smile that bursts without rage. Shrinks,
Then settles, sweetened, like an obelisk.
Then a miracle of reaching, without risk.
I can't do it. It would take my mother's strength.

1621–1627
Villon

Vivisectious frost, vivacious wind, my bread is baked.
I'm shocked, like Margot. Like us all.
Like angels, like Villon: we're praying naked.
Like a rat trap needs a rat to maul
Open-mouthed. We're on our knees, wine-soaked,
No stopping Time. We choke
Giving each other meat and drink here in our Hall.

Three

TO LOVE THROWN LIKE A ROPE

The sun smacks the room in the early afternoon.
The sex between the two drunk lovers has just stopped.
Their situations are desperate in real life. Too soon
It will have to be real again. Now, while he stares, she talks.

Just bite a stick, they used to say, you're only bleeding.
They listen to *Cocksucker Blues'*
Viral tin sounds. She gets up and starts chopping
Red meat and chopping basil into smaller bits. He chews

His lip and watches the Firefly Lady, "Mrs. Schmelling,"
In the credits. Are you into this decade? Couldn't anyone get crocked
Enough tonight to say into a phone, "everything's
Good," and mean it? O Man, just don't say it was just bad luck

After you let them make it a world of prose. All
The poor old world is watched by the beady-eyed. Each small
Air-conditioner a lung, each naked groupie shooting dope
One more time Frank could have been showing "Loving Cup."

Each argument the lovers have so like a crack-head Pan
Thrash-dancing in each chest. O Life, garnished with rancid tripe.
As if the air they breathe is evil acid, meat pie flan,
A field of wasps and cream in each one's windpipe.

"It's what I *have* to do," Mick Jagger whispers as he rasps
In his harmonica. He is a bullet, he's been fired and flies.
She is a solar system cutting meat. He needs to clasp
Her not to drown. O Lord, they bow, and rise.

Accept this, pin it through another angel's cheek. Forbear
And we'll eat gratefully what's chopped. "It's what I *have* to do."
The sun makes him swear. She turns around, not scared.
The light comes in and in. "It's what I *have* to do."

DILETTANTES

Sleeping dirt muck in my eyes and a chest full of rheum
And caramels. One day none of us would make curios

Of what our Muses whispered anymore. Beastly it is to hang an ugly story
On someone. People beastly drunk, just foxed,

Each Christmas. Let their minds become just porridge
Bowls of horseflies in molasses. So instead

Of West Point cadets lined up for graduation,
There are expensive rooms full of white hornets

Flecked with carbine grey. A warped vinyl soundtrack
Of what was inscribed on a scabbard.

Minds like rich kids throwing plums at cars,
Laughing when one wrecks.

DINNER PARTY IN THE SOUTH: A VISION

"Now . . . now . . . now!" —Jackson Pollock

Dinner is being prepared. So drunk you're wobbling
You sit down. Sounds as though they're squabbling

In the kitchen and to lighten it you quip,
"They're giving a pig a rough time of it

In there." One glares at your boots, but no one laughs.
You notice when they talk about the past

It's like they're each walking a dog around
A giant porcelain bowl, so spread apart not one

Can hear another. You cough and see a little barf
On your sleeve. You're not sure this is smart.

You eat some nuts. Happiness is a choice. "Allow me,"
Says your aunt, proffering your uncle's tie.

"He's always paid too much for nuts," she says.
"They're way too high." Your uncle says

If she hits his nose again he'll hit her
Back. "Oh, is that your nose?" she says. "Your nuts're

So high I thought that thing was your dick." "I wish I'd not been
Born," you say, forlorn. "Don't say that, Angel,"

Says your aunt. "It was a happy minute for us
All when you were born."

DAMNED

In an empty church you shake like the hands
Of your cancer-sick Mom that fall. Your plan

To be a sage, spend your life irritated
At other people, feel deflated

And elated all at once reciting a new poem,
Failed. You feel surrounded, like you'd blow 'em

All away if it were legal. When you turned
In bed and dreamed you swung, you turned

In bed and wrapped the sheets around
Yourself and heard the crows sound

Their joyful appetites on your shoulder.
She saw your face just then, she who'd gotten older

With you, told you later you looked wonderful,
And that she loved you more. Your past is full

Of snows and swagger. Your dead are real,
They're on your shoulders, picking at your meals.

MEDICINE SHOW

The first Stones albums had lots of covers. In Texas,
Growing up—or rolling up—I knew
The Stones weren't poets but magicians, seeing
Lovesome sparrows and many moons, like me,
While everyone else sat jobless, worthless
And unreal in a Cadillac or Lexus, coming home
From banks. Stop peeing yourself, Nut. Buttercup
Wants her lower lip in my mouth, not in yours.
You're the last of four on her list. And no matter how hard
You polish that Toyota, those thoughts appearing
To you when rain beads as you drive won't be
The words to your new novel or a revelation about government.

IT HAPPENS

I think, "Her thigh's a little bruised,"
Before I kiss her mouth. It never happens.
I only think it. She looks up and says the sky

Looks bruised. She says, *goddamn, the sky*
Looks bruised. She walks away to get some wine
And I think, "The backs of her calves are perfect

For that remark." She comes back with the wine
And I'm about to quote something when she sees
My book and says, *shitting poetry, what a French*

Thing to do: it's Life dropped at you by someone
Who's already used it. My senses and my feelings
Are a little bruised. Who is she to mouth off

At my book? "Don't whine," I tell myself.
I'm getting a little drunk, and want to kiss her
Thigh—bruised or not. It doesn't happen.

It's just a thought. "Happen," I moan, sotto voce,
Looking down. "Thought, wish you'd just happen."
You're talking to yourself, she says. I'm drunk

With bruises. The sky is bruised. My feelings are bruised.
My book is the shit of someone French. My Life
Is getting used. It's happening! It's happening!

SEVERAL HISTORIES

freely after Hikmet

One cannot love more than one other
With the fierceness of the love one torn
Half has for another. One cannot be a piece

Of memory ripped from a life, one cannot love
More than one other truly.

What a lie—
It happens all the time. Joy, Molly, Kelly

Davenport sophomore year. A white path lies
Before me. I decide it's I-35
South, to Waxahachie, Waco, Austin,
I must be going to Padre Island. Maybe my

Beloved is in a field of bluebonnets on the way. Kelly used to kick
Her shoes off carefully and we could see her toes.
For Someone Lucky's sake the toes were perfect, enough
Said. If only I could find that girl, who wore the salmon
Colored skirt and small white top, who had the red hair
And who—hell, if I could just find her I would forget
About the first one, back in Dallas, who when I kissed her
Just there, just on her left shoulder,

Laughed aloud and into being came three worlds
Where I still live. The women I love
                    Are laughing and crying at once, in two
Or maybe three languages. How are you all here? You don't
Even watch the same things on tv, how can you all
Be here?

Every morning just before I wake up, I dream
Of a woman,
                    and I *love* her, man,
                                        I wake up and try to email her
RIGHT THEN, and I blaze through the shit, shave, and bathe
Routine and roll out, grab a taxi, tell him, "get there, brother, go!"

"Go where?" he says . . .

EMBERS OF AN ODE

She says it to herself but he can hear it.

"The King marries dawn," he thinks. "He doesn't marry sunset."

FATHER TO SON

Like Odysseus to his son, I'd like to pray
And have it reach him. And I'd like to hit
The light switch in his room eight minutes
Early, cover my laughter at his groans,

And say, "Wake up and piss! The world's on fire!"
The Lord of Hosts is with us.

This vision is a ticklish thing, a feather
Near some snoring giant's nose, be
Careful with it. All war is a web of men,
Not just a flash of your temper.

Think your anger will bring superior force to bear?
Hell, David got Goliath with a rock.

———

Dad was born in Peking, China, where Kewpie
Was stationed. He and Grandmother Yuill
Lived there for years.

He breaketh the bow, and cutteth the spear
In sunder. He burneth the chariot in the fire.

———

"Mr. Yuill, you know where you are?"
"Yes."

46

"Will you tell us, sir?"
"Baylor Hospital, Dallas, Texas."

He might have had sleep apnea, he might have had
Cheyne-Stokes respiration. To check, the doctors
Asked him questions, checked his mind.

"Sir, have you ever been in the hospital before?"
"The last time I was in a hospital
Was in Peking, China, and I only went
That time to see my parents."

———

Funny thing about that, I said at his funeral,
Giving his eulogy, is that the doctors didn't get it.
From the back filled with lawyers he'd practiced with,
Loud guffaws, men slapping their knees.

I shall be exalted among the heathen,
I shall be exalted in the earth.

Dad died at sixty-nine. He worked himself
To death helping people with no money.
The heathens were not those who didn't go to church,
They were those who made and kept the money,
Those for whom the world was there to be
Conquered. Dad thought the world should be saved.

———

When Jacob wrestles an angel, or Tumlinson
Fights a Comanche, each is struggling
With himself. Each war is quicksand
For the guy who thinks he's a cat,
Is soldiering for him who thinks he's a poet
Dreaming he's a soldier. Vision is ticklish,
Tom. It leads you into caves where you wake
Giants who don't care about your vision.

He maketh wars to cease unto the end of the earth.

Look up from your raft on the Rio Grande.
The Harrah-Hamarrah are looking down from
The cliff above. Tom, it may be you will survive,
But only by bowing your head.

There is a river, the streams whereof
Shall make glad the city of God.

You're a good boy, Tom, he said once
As I tidied up his hospital room.

I shall be exalted among the heathen,
I shall be exalted in the earth.
The Lord of Hosts is with us;
The God of Jacob is our refuge. Selah.

Four

TO THE SOUND OF A STRING AS IT SNAPS

I.

William Bonney, after the death of John Tunstall

That week I figured I was done.
Who could be worth a damn to anyone
who feels this old? Watching one

of my teeth that just fell out,
which didn't make sense, the punch wasn't that hard,

I figured, let that string you thought held on
To one more chance for you just snap.
There's no more chances for the likes of me.

And it was not a dream. That string was there
Connecting me with something like a life. I had it, and when it got broke

For real, I figured as I sat there spitting out torn bits of bits of gum
And spitting everything,

        that chance has been cut off
In real life, you should cut it off inside as well, Bill.
This world is not for I.

What if you survived long past
The point where you could both survive and make it back?
Not like returning from a place, but like restoring what was yours

Inside yourself, what got torn out.
What if you can still believe in life, but it
Just isn't there, your life just isn't there, and isn't coming back?

Isn't that the moment when you're free?

2.

Telemachus to Athena, *The Odyssey, Book III*

Stranger, at this point, I just try not to fear
The bewildering night, or the slothful
Afternoons, hollow in the hollow light.
The shade in my mind is thick
As a stone wall, the shade in my mind
Is thick with medicinal smell.
Yesterday, head in my hands, I thought
My venerable father was standing nearby.
   I hold him in my heart the way the lion's
Head holds the iron ring on the door
Of the venerable building. He said he is
Always with me, and I believed him.
But today, still, nothing is the same.
And today, still, it seems my fault.

3.

The green sea in my bad mind keeps bursting, drifting away,
Then swelling up again. For three days now,
My image of myself has been a bat
Slung around in a sack. Technically I flew,
But I was being flung much more. It's true,
I wasn't protein, then, my friend. I wound up
Being barfed. I dropped into Hell with a splat.
You know what? No one else was there.

4.

The rat in that feedbag keeps growing.
Not knowing what song he shall sing before he dies
Is the one job almost anyone can get.
Through fields of crosses, through pursed lips, the verses
All amount to: maybe, maybe not.
She says, "See my Bosnian license plates?"
He says, "You can come see me if you can get past my dogs."

MEDICINE SHOW

In Coolidge, Texas, where he finally agreed to be buried,
We rolled up, one cilia after another boiling dread
Where gravestone prayers should have been. You're a magician
If you can see hoot owls, moons, and such. I'm washing
Mom's Cadillac for her, because me sitting
Next to her as she, tears streaming, said, "well your
Dad loves you, Tom," was me beginning at last.
Of four thoughts he had the day he died
The last was this: "you're a good boy, Tom."
The last words she had said when she died
Were, "yes, I love you, too."

DEBATE WITH HIS HEART

Villon

Who's there? "It's me. Your heart." What heart?
"We need to talk." Well? "I'm hanging on here by a thread.
I'm losing succor, low on blood,
It hurts. You're cloistered, torn apart,
And sulking in a corner like a cur."
What causes that? "Your mad pursuit of pleasures."
What is that to you? "Man, I'm in seizures."
Then leave. "I can't." All right, I'll listen—
"When?" When my heartlessness is cured.
"I've tried to warn you." Thanks, I've tried to listen.

"What's your plan?" To be worthwhile some day.
"You're over thirty now." The mule's pissed away
His salad days? "You're either childish or depressed."
Indentured, not indented, since you ask. Oh, and I'm stressed.
"You don't know much, do you?" I do. Two flies in milk,
One black, the other white, are not the same.
"You done?" I like your long-eared, braying game.
"If this won't work, I'll start again:
You're lost." I always find myself hauling ass uphill.
"I've tried to warn you." Thanks, I've tried to listen.

"I've the gripe here, you're giving me pain.
Were you ignorant, or already a goner,
Or just stupid—any decent reason would bear
Scrutiny. But you don't care. You act like *foul* and *fair*

Are the same thing. Either you're a box of rocks
Or pain delights you more than honor.
I think you love pain. Well? Why won't you talk?"
It'll all be left behind me when I'm gone.
"God! Some comfort." It's the only explanation.
"I'm trying to warn you." Thanks, I'm trying to listen.

"Why are you so sad?" I've had bad luck.
I think when Saturn packed my satchel
He put these troubles in. "That's crazy talk;
You're Saturn's lord, but you talk like his servant.
On this, remember Solomon's account:
'A wise man,' he writes, 'has authority
Over the planets' sway. Wisdom makes him free.'"
I think not; my hand's dealt, I play.
"What?" You heard it: my philosophy.
"I'm trying to help you." Thanks, I'm trying to listen.

"Vow to live like this, huh?" God grant me the strength.
"If you do, you'll need—" What? "—a twinge of conscience,
Lots of books—" Which books? "—some literature, and think:
Less time spent with fools might help, too." I'll think about it.
"Oh, no you won't." I will. Now, will I change? I doubt it—
"Nothing good will come of living just on whims.
I've tried to warn you." Thanks. I've tried to listen.

QUATRAINS

Hikmet

Every person everyone meets will always be
An enemy, a lover, or a friend. A window opens
You didn't see, and souls stream into memory
And beg, "love this one, treat that one as a friend."

Biting the firm apple's white curved flesh
One February day, crystalline with yearning. Love,
This world will melt, but we'll drift in our dervish
Of sharpening joy. Breath in the cold. Pine branches above.

Perhaps we could never have loved with such force
Without, from a distance, each marveling first
That the other's soul was the torn half we lived for.
Perhaps we had to wander, desperate, first.

Now the day has drained away completely.
All its dregs sunk to muffled night.
Beloved, when we meet in our sleepy, wasted clarity
What I see is a holy, almost unbearable light . . .

AH! BIRTHDAY!

Figure of Grace, tickler of enzymes. I'd run behind
Without you, barking for reprieve. Run mad around
The soldiers standing on parade, instead of chopping
Backstroke style through weathery mornings,
Drunk with love. This is the Year of The Curved
Behind. Those red dots are the maw, yawning at us,
From behind the still unwritten eulogies. This is the smile
You brought up the Eiffel Tower for me. When you're away
I see bluish daggers flying toward a librarian, I am made
Of reprehensible smoke. I think I belong in this one,
You said once. Write me in, please, and I do,
As an obelisk blowing baby spiders out the window,
Into the breeze.

FRAGMENT

from Leopardi

Above, atop the old tower,
As long as daylight lasts, you sing,
The sound a swirling, less a maelstrom
Than a dream of song that fills my room.

MADE OF CORAL

1.

AH, to be corpuscular and jagged, a coral
Shaped by the movement of the water
And living at an unusual, slow speed,
And an occurrence in the movement
Of the water, a moment in the life
Of someone else, someone who watches,
Leaning here, just here, above me.

2.

Again, the dust I swept already, and again
The fuzz fronds, the weird smearing
Of that color, red, on my bed.
My mind's gone all corpuscular, the hands
Are red which grope it, it's torn,
Not anti-marriage.

3.

He knows the
Red spots will be cancerous.
She knows nobody really talks until
She leaves the room. No happiness
Like theirs was ever painted in the caves
In France.

4.

Snow lands on their scalped heads, speeds the little ones to Hell.
Fire-colored light shines between their ribs and cleans,
A salt wash in her mouth, a heart still flopping. Smell
The bodies being boiled. Or were they sharecropped?
Shaped by corpuscular muses, a wave or an ember catching.
A color, like a kid pissed there. Fuzz fronds smearing
Their pale hands on my Beloved's heart. Tap and grind
Of little teeth gnawing a lamp cord. The gift is *was*,
The gift is *beyond*.

BALLADE

for Leslie Lee

As it twists as it grows,
A yearning in bloom,
This lilac wrings
From the singing sun
Something between sleepy
Lust and ancient whispered prayer.
Part wet kiss, part naked
Lover under the moon.
I am always naked with you,
We are always asleep
In the hands of the Lord.
That you smile and speak
Softly is the history of a star.
That you laugh aloud
Alone in the bath
Is gypsies raising their song,
Drinking all night,
Playing at dice
While it snows.

VERITAS

for Leslie Lee

Imagining Heaven as Istanbul, or a beach south of Istanbul,
Where your friends are preparing an apartment for you
And your Beloved. And sleeping fathers, babies plump
And shining as good faith, memory in the faithful heat.
You and she in the fastening-unfastenings of heat. And poetry
Just capers in the leafy thoughts above. Just Orpheus exhausted
Now but coughing little plaints. Just memory rewritten,
Honey, just like Louis Armstrong's voice, like some
Big happy face. Just living, living, Honey, just believe,
Don't understand so much. Just come to bed, she says.

NOTES

"Bit: An Ode with the Rolling Stones Playing in the Background": Line 9 is from the song "Shattered," written by Mick Jagger and Keith Richards.

"Ode to the Wind": The phrase "swirl and vortex" is borrowed from Larry Levis.

The Hikmet, Corbiere, and Villon poems are not always meant to be translations, but imitations, soundings out loud of guiding whispers the poet keeps hearing as he endures the medicine show. Rosanna Warren has my profound thanks for her inspiration and help with Villon. The Hikmet would not be possible without the help of Mehmet Bozacioglu.

"Dallas Skinheads": Class-related statements in rock and roll were generally misunderstood and transformed by Texas listeners into stylistic preferences. Behavior accompanied stylistic choices. The four quoted lines are from the song "Streets of Laredo."

"To Love Thrown Like a Rope": Robert Frank was retained by the Rolling Stones to make a film of their 1972 tour of America. Rather than focusing on the music—arguably the best rock and roll ever played—Frank made a memorable film about deteriorating culture.

"Dinner Party in the South: A Vision": The parts about the pig and someone having a happy minute when I was born are borrowed freely from Harvard Lampoon's often terrible *Bored of the Rings*.

"Father to Son": Tumlinson was a Texas Ranger during the nineteenth century. Kewpie is the nickname by which we all knew my grandfather, Colonel Charles Walter Yuill. Cheyne-Stokes respiration can be caused by a brainstem stroke. The patient suffers periods of irregular breathing, with an attendant irregular heartbeat. One symptom is loss of memory.

"To the Sound of a String as It Snaps": William Bonney, or "Billy the Kid," had been abandoned by his stepfather after the death of his mother, and traveled for a while in the company of outlaws. He had returned to New Mexico and found gainful employment with John Tunstall. Tunstall's death at the hands of men hired by his business competitors prompted Bonney to become a "regulator"—a member of a rival gang whose pursuit of justice involved, essentially, a string of homicides, during which he became very famous as a gunslinger. Telemachus, believing he is talking to a stranger, is making a confession to Athena.

"Debate with His Heart": The refrain line was inspired by Robert Pinsky.